IDIOT VERSE

IDIOT VERSE

KEATON HENSON

B
G S
P

THE **BLACK SPRING**
PRESS GROUP

First published in 2015
Second printing in 2016
Third printing in 2022
by Black Spring Press Group
Suite 38, 19-21 Crawford Street
London, W1H 1PJ
United Kingdom

Cover design and illustrations by Keaton Henson
Typeset by Edwin Smet
Author photograph by Sophie Harris-Taylor

ISBN 978-1-908998-84-2

BLACKSPRINGPRESSGROUP.COM

KEATON HENSON

is a musician, writer and visual artist from the suburbs
of London, England.

He has released three critically-acclaimed albums:
Dear..., *Birthdays*, and *Romantic Works* as well
as scoring for ballet and film.

Keaton has also shown his art in exhibitions around
the world and published a book called *Gloaming*.

He is currently finishing work on his fourth album
alongside new exhibitions and books.

Table of Contents

your life is a book
it is more than its first and last page
and is mostly made up of 'and's and 'the's

Idiot Verse

dear reader,
  please read as though sleeping
  I'm aware I will not be the first
to write stanzas of rhyme of my loneliness
  but here is my idiot verse

no, it's not meant to be clever or wise
  it is feelings penned just as I've seen them
and how can the lines be affecting your soul
  when you're too busy reading between them

so I'll write it out just as I see it
  and just as it sounds in my heart
and pay no mind to those wasting their time
  in confusing confusion with art

Grow Up With Me

grow up with me
let's run in fields and fear the dark together
fall off swings and burn special things
and both play outside in bad weather

let's eat badly
let's watch adults drink wine and laugh at their idiocy
let's sit in the back of the car
making eye contact with strangers driving past
making them uncomfortable
not caring, not swearing, don't fuck

let's both reclaim our superpowers
the ones we all have and lose with our milk teeth
the ability not to fear social awkwardness
to panic when locked in the cellar
still sure there's something down there
and while picking from pillows each feather
let's both stay away from the edge of the bed
forcing us closer together

let's sit in public, with ice cream all over both our faces
sticking our tongues out at passers by
let's cry
let's swim
let's everything

let's not find it funny lest someone falls over
classical music is boring
poetry baffles us both
as nothing that's said is what's meant
plays are long, tiresome, sullen and filled…

with hours that could be spent rolling down hills
and grazing our knees on cement

let's hear stories and both lose our innocence
learn about parents and forgiveness
death and morality
kindness and art
thus losing both of our innocent hearts
but at least we won't do it apart

grow up with me

Hell

hell is a lonely deathbed
heaven, good friends to leave behind
and life my dear, is a fleeting affair
so why not spend your one, in mine

I'm With You

my dearest reader, writer, kin
though I try to let you in
I am much too scared to speak
in my tone so small and meek

so I utter in the voices
(as though I have no other choices)
of the ones who spoke to me
when I grew and learned to read

men and women just like us
full of woe and fear and lust
broken eyes and skinny wrists
yellow caffeine fingertips

stammers, lisps and broken bones
childhoods softly spent alone
inky marks upon their faces
awkward schoolyard second bases

but they grew to how I found them
gods now free of all that bound them
seeming, dreaming poets all
born to rise and bound to fall

and I knew I'd never be
alone again and I was free
so I spent my days at home
with my heroes all alone

we're the ones they think are strange
we're the ones the kids rename
damn it yes, I'm one of them
down with normal raise your pen

so now on quiet London days
whether or not I'm getting paid
I do what my heroes do
and cannot help but think of you

so if you're told you aren't right
and you are too weak to fight
know that as you sit and read
I'm with you if you're with me

On Touring

must you stare my crooked darlings
can't you see the words I say
mean nothing since the day I wrote them
all you see is farce today

don't applaud me well-meant watchers
I am tired and struggle just
walking from behind the curtain
but have bills and so I must

please don't make me wicked strangers
I mean only to create
but am stifled by my travels
frightened still from date to date

must you stare so, foreign lovers
can't you see the dance I do
is rehearsed and slowly stiffens
but if I must
I'll dance for you

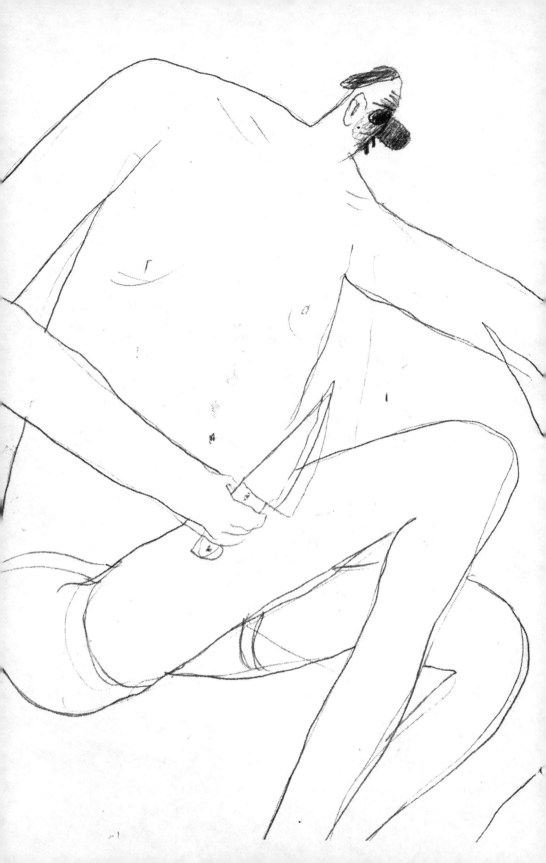

The Pugilist

down with the artist fighting death
dirty hair and laboured breath
swampy blues that go for days
sleeping pills and masquerades

bless the agents fighting fees
wounds from days spent on their knees
living in the modern age
damn the critic burn the page

tip the barman feeding gin
to the writer peeling skin
from his withered fingertips
half-writ poems on his lips

cruel desires, thirst for fame
naming books and naming names
fuck the i's and fuck the dots
long live the publisher, down with the plot

up with the editor cut it to shreds
outdated words from suffering heads
mark of the lunatic, sign of the cross
far too much rhyming, self-loathing dross

pray for the painter asleep on the floor
missing the party, acting the whore
dreaming of love again, dreaming of much
losing the battle and losing your touch

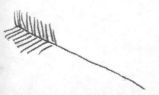

weep for the artisan writing the psalm
carving a verse in the back of his arm
send for the troubadour bring me his head
write till your fingers bleed write till you're dead

long live the king in the street holding court
talking to strangers and building a fort
mourn for the songwriter up in the night
god bless the pugilist throwing the fight

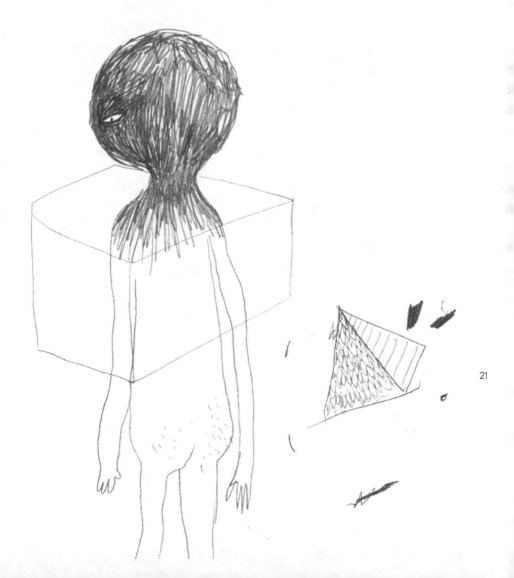

Hiding It

I'll hide it from you all
and keep it to myself
lest you think me bedlam bound
and hide from me as well

I vow to stow it all away
and keep the world from you
if I can't handle all of it
how could you feel it to?

so I'll smoke a cigarette and think
of everything you are
how can I feed and dress myself
while thinking of the stars?

Polite Plea

come and be human with me
eat nothing that means us both leaving the house
sit on the floor in strange places
and sleep in familiar beds

I will make art, not for, but about you
speak truths while you're sleeping and wake you with hands
we will dive deeply into one another
and stay out of our own weary heads

we will argue in glorious fireworks
I will throw words, you will break my guitar
remind ourselves that it's something worth burning
and be all the better for making up

come and eat cereal late at night
in silence, undressed on the kitchen floor
be far too tired for tomorrow's long stroll
in love, just enough for the waking up

come in your own time, and human be

yours politely,
lonely me

The One

you are the one for me
make me feel young
take me on holiday
bite off my tongue

darling one, darling
there's nothing you lack
I'll give you the sky
or the skin off my back

you are my angel
I'll keep you from harm
talk to me sweetly
break both my arms

my Aphrodite
you're every breath
sing me a lullaby
love me to death

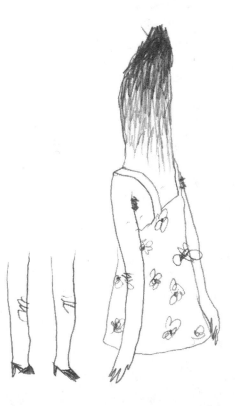

Cumulus

I sent a cloud
it looked all sweet in snow light
too cold for morning dew
I sent it from my window
in hopes it would find you

I sent a cloud
from window over frosty ground
soft and all afloat
with grey upon its linings
like waves upon a boat

I sent a cloud
in hope that it would find you
and kiss you as you woke
and if it does please overlook
the fact it's made of smoke

Duvet Dancing

selfless lovers may stare at clouds
and whisper prose in soft, clean ears
but I selfish itch and dream and hear
of you and I dancing in duvets my dear

listen, white rabbit, Brooklyn-bound
care, care less, come care for me
I live restless all for thee
come, let's be normal, I'll make tea

I lay still sick, ill of chairs
restless is as restless seems
limbs frenetic, swarms of bees
unable to finish movies

longing for you, in longer hours
knowing you still live in daylight
preemptively I sit and write
of all our duvet dancing nights

Smoke Signals

I'm smoking a lot
and starting to doubt
if I'm breathing you in
or smoking you out

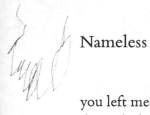

Nameless

you left me somehow from afar
through this pixelated cage
O wonders of the modern age
my nameless has a nameless grace

I quickly switched to standby heart
and sat for hours in waking dreams
for all in love is all it seems
my nameless loves in nameless dreams

the room in which I live and work
void of any rarity
now is travelled over seas
my nameless has no name for me

and how at once with clicks and taps
can such a tie be fully cut
so coldly can our book be shut
my nameless named my loathsome guts

the ghost remains in folders here
but tells me strongly 'she is free'
but, please know you'll always be
my nameless love unloving me

Regret Me

who watches while you dance my dear?
who whispers softly 'are you well?'
and softer still in moonlight's spell
'I'm lonely my love, come and save me'

who listens to your collars turn
your sleeves drip red as arms and hands
reach, desperate, for escaping sands?
I'm lonely my darling, don't break me

here's this, just this to keep in mind
the times we had and how I left
us both behind and so bereft

I'm lonely my dear, forget me.
I'm lonely, pretend that you left me
I'm lonely, so please just let me

be alone,
but regret me

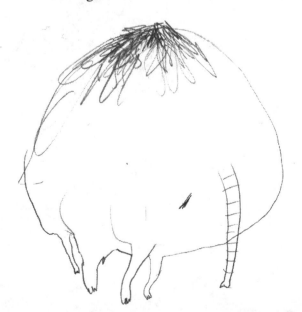

Moon Bride

my bride the moon though she strains my eyes
looks down on me and will watch as I die
she helps the night come and the tides to drift
my bride the moon works the nightshift

An Argument

there's beauty in the breakup
and love within the taunts
years of life are dredged to land
from all their ancient haunts

blame has acid on its tongue
but sweetness in intent
words of all the words unspoke
in loving hours spent

clothes unfolded cast to air
like wings upon the starling
don't say words you may regret
and don't throw plates my darling

such highly human poetry
is uttered at the door
when she names he a piece of shit
and he names she a whore

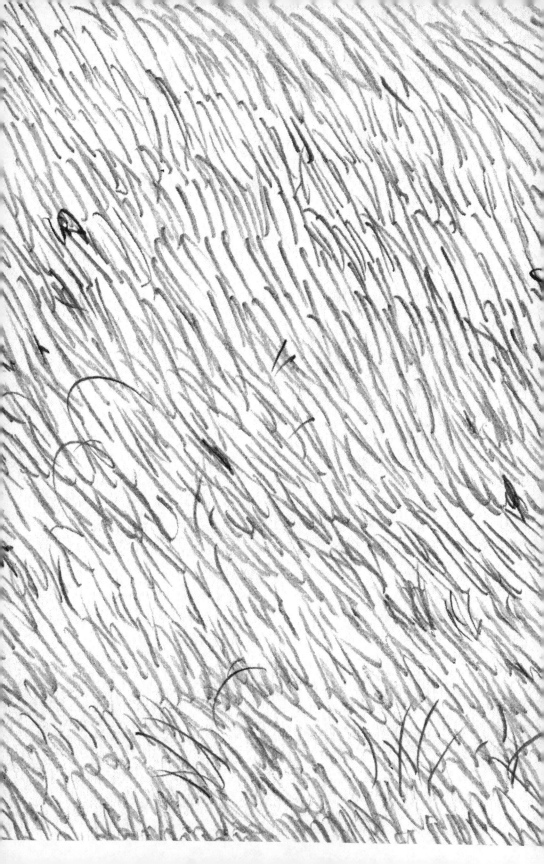

Los Angeles Rental

just to let you know

your house is broken
I used your house and broke all the things
you see, when you said 'no strings'
I took that to mean I could use your things
as I would use my own
which often leads to breakage
for reasons quite unknown
though you can ask the neighbours
I was quiet as a mouse
and didn't set the place alight
sorry I broke your house

p.s don't turn on the oven

Too Soon

I know
I left you far too soon my love
but knew from every laugh
that I was never going to be
able to be enough

I know I gave up far too soon
and left in a loathsome way
but please understand I'm not quite a man
but perhaps will be someday

I miss you dearly and sorely wish
our time was as we'd planned
but I ran and hid too soon to tell
what we both had in hand

please write me songs my love and then
it will not be in vain
they do not need to sing my praise
or even say my name

but if you can please don't forget
though do not feel bereft
do you remember the time you raised your voice
and I got scared and left?

Heirlooms

that's where we stood
when I said I loved you and you said it too
that's where we stood when we cried through a winter
and I wrote the songs that I thought were for you

that's where we laughed
laughed at the people all happy in May
that's where we groaned at the dancing and drinking
all through the year before you went away

that's where we walked
when I told you darling I can't bear to sing
that's where we walked when the moon told us stories
stories about almost everything

that's where we sat
I at my writing and you on the phone
that's where we sat as we bickered like children
I don't tend to sit there now I am alone

here's where we lay
here where I still try to sleep and to write
here where you uttered a name I knew dearly
told me you loved him and left in the night

Nightdrinking

dream of the evening
wake in the morning
call for a taxi and leave in disgust
t-shirt on backwards and hair in a mess
all for fucking in fucking we trust
lost in the grief, baying for teeth
good grief
good heavens
good lust

Bloodline

the way
the way they say I haven't washed my hair
or eaten well today
makes family, family, more than just they
more than just favours and dues
payment for shoes
a home with ten legs gladly following you

they will cook
they will cook for you if you are hungry
or give you a bed that smells partly of yours
partly of theirs as you are
allow you to eat in their car
wear rubber gloves when you're lost and in love
interrupt you on phones from afar

the place
the place in itself is irrelevant
and almost an insult to the word
family's family, and happy to be
when you are silently watching TV
hearing old stories and falling asleep
they are the only thing keeping you free
love them in spite of the faults you can see
but when you do, do not come and tell me
tell them

constantly

Louise

Louise lives in heaven
her kindly voice ringing through wood panelled walls
out of the window
down through the valley
and mingles in forests with fox calls

I play piano
the notes harmonising with hissing of snow
passing through woods
over the roads
mixing with tunes from a decade ago

there's tea when you waken
every morning in croaking we settle the scores
on through the leaves
over the fields
sneaking through cracks in the door

the treehouse is still only started
it's been that way since I was here at age seven
as with my kin
letting me in
my cousin Louise lives in heaven

Sanctuary

as we drive past Lower Slaughter
I feel the nearness, just a quarter
of a mile to Henson Farm
kindly words and loving arms

lifting dead sheep over fences
softly as the day commences
then back home to quiet tea
wine for you and calm for me

late night walks with full bright torches
mornings spent on quiet porches
I wake softly, cigarette
loving family no regrets

Lou leaves ashtrays on the tables
I help out when I am able
they know life is time to kill
hate the habit, love me still

in the evening music enters
through the windows from the centre
of the woods where foxes sing
and birds beat rhythms with their wings

deer play horns and call for lovers
I write poems under cover
of a quilt in musty heap
then drift perfect, off to sleep

as we drive past Lower Slaughter
past the stagnant lake of water
I turn back to see them small
goodbye Woodhouse, cousins all

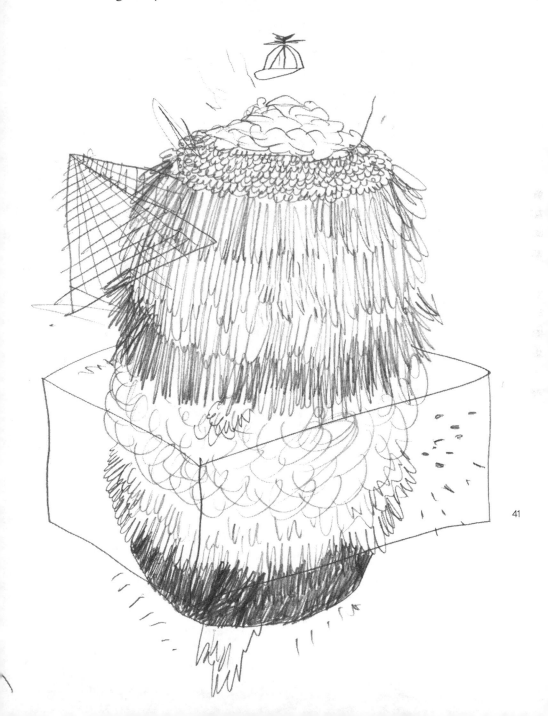

Richmond

Richmond, you weirdo, I love you to death
tell me of history, spent in your breadth
tell me of loves that were made in your parks
and then in your coffee shops, broken apart

teach me of how it must feel to be home
and love a place so much you're never alone
to take it for granted, and walk in its days
but need it like sleeping when you've gone away

it's summer now, tell, is your grass turned to brown
and how many prams are being wheeled through the town?
have ice creams been dropped on your better-days paving
and how are the afternoon pub-drunks behaving?

town hall, please chime for me, tell me you care
send it cacophonous into the air
sing to the bend of the river below
your crumbling clock tower, peppered with crows

does the Thames still course through you and wearily wave
bringing the sad news from London each day?
does it still stop for a minute to breathe
before moving so gloomily, on to the sea?

and how are the birds, are they keeping awake
all of the businessmen up until late?
are some dogs still howling late into the night
mourning the loss of the daylight?

Excursions

no more staying indoors
there are battles to build and cities to burn
carpets to muddy and waking to earn
someone's to something, and somethings to learn
come now, no more staying indoors

there'll be no more staying indoors
less of the longing, the ardent lust
more of the breathing, in breathing we trust
more of the beating of hearts in the dusk
no more staying indoors

here now, no more staying indoors
there are fears to a'frighten and pockets to fill
dreams for forgetting and hopes to be killed
words to be written, and written but still
it's awfully warm here indoors

Big Smoke

goodbye North Sheen, hello Barnes
four stops to Waterloo, sound the alarm

good evening Underground, off to the East
used to be eel and mash, now artists in heat

wave to the Oxo, Clapham's a mess
dodge the commuters, rigid with stress

ads for the theatre, men on the tracks
moan of delays again, long journey back

eyes to the pavement, Oxford Street's filled
surrounded by people, lonelier still

Bay Bridge

hold tight my dear creature we're leaving
off on a ride to the end of the world
on through the trees
over the seas
onwards to where the buildings burn
past mockingbirds cursing our foolishness
and ants building cities with crumbs

here, see the faces confused and in awe
cursing us both as we pass
it's burning my darling
isn't it beautiful?
don't you wish there was a camera at hand?
or anyone left alive in the land
to hear us tell how it went down?
oh and how I wish we could be found

together we'd be, in the ashes
a symbol too late of the hope that we had
hope for me
hope for the rest
watch as the whole world's eyes shut
but see through their lids as they pass
the familiar warmth and glowing
as though back in the womb at last

On England

farewell curdled England
forget I existed
wave me goodbye with the wind through the trees
always consensual
never insisted
is my love for you and is your love for me

how I miss woodland
rivers and chimneys
trains full of coughing and sneezing and talk
breath always visible
arthritic trees
as me and the Thames take a long quiet walk

and London you blight on the
landscape, I love you
a festering, rain sodden, beautiful hive
send me the filthiest
bird from above you
just to assure me that you're still alive

farewell scent of salty damp
smoke and stale toffee
visions of pale beauty wrapped up in scarves
here we go, window seat
aeroplane coffee
goodbye to cold nights indoors in warm baths

farewell my darling
watch as I disappear
try, in my absence to not come undone
sing to me wistfully
I will be here
in an LA apartment besieged by the sun

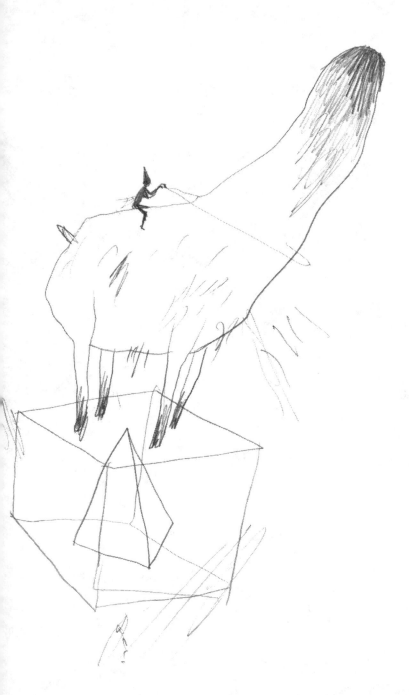

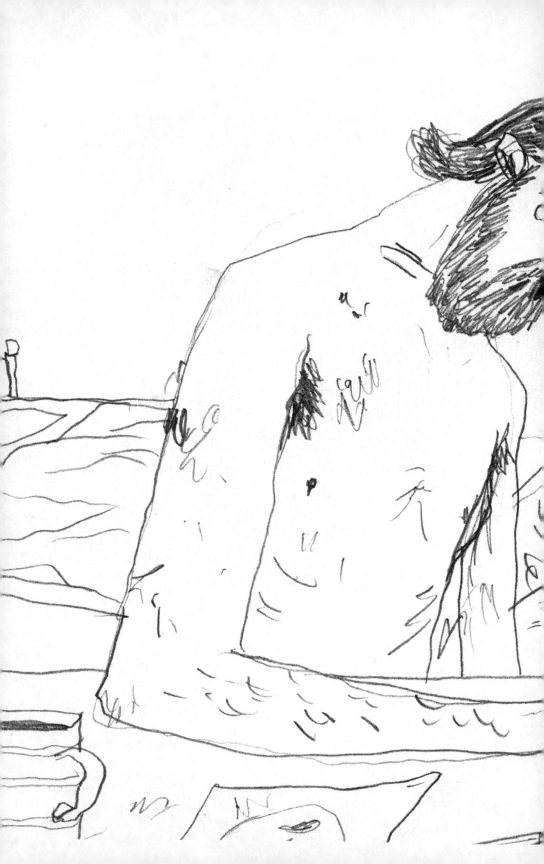

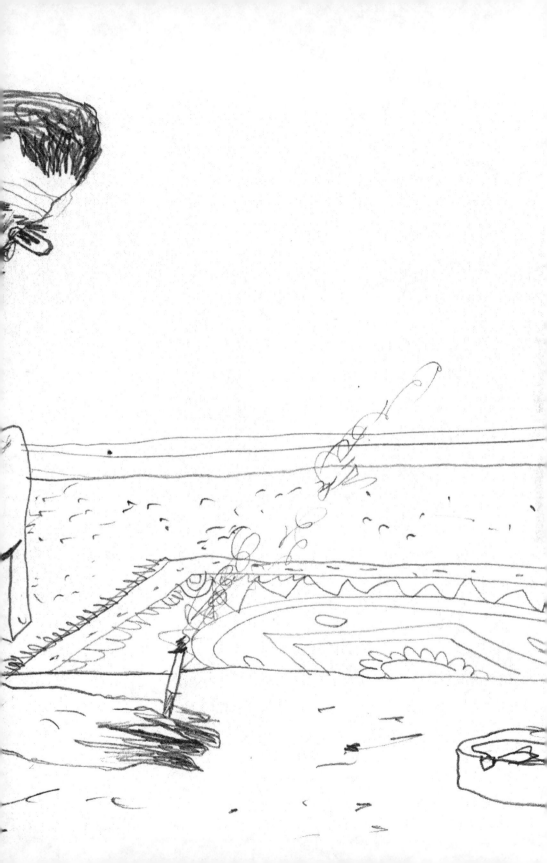

All The Wings

...such was the day only trees recall
when ash grew on the plain
and all the wings of all the insects
fell to earth like rain

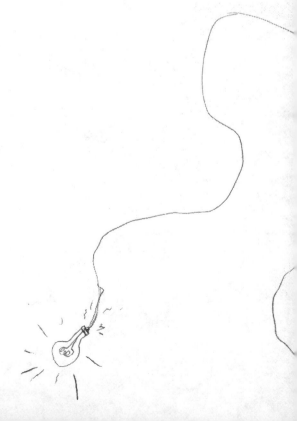

The Nandy Oak

dying dance on cupboards walk
regard the marbled crow
read the throats of peregrines
scared of all the snow

sing daily to the nandy oak
to hope the fork will clay
ankle salt upon your dove
and oceans far away

Leaving It Behind

tonight I will think about nothing
for once I shall empty my head
but if I'm to spend my life rhyming
will you rhyme for me when I am dead?

will you sing to the trees I existed,
tell the rivers they're wasting their time?
if I stay here a couple more weeks love
will you tell the whole world I was fine?

if I build up a workload to leave here
will you make sure it's read when I go?
if there's no one to love me while living
who's there to let them all know?

will you write out my name on a banner
and parade it and yell in the streets
that someone on earth once existed
that none of them ever will meet?

if they don't care please play them my songs love
perhaps then at least they can hear
that even if scores are not mourning the loss
perhaps I once had a good ear

so it's 3 o'clock in the morning
and I still haven't emptied my mind
and this poem is not quite a masterpiece
but at least I can leave it behind

Insomnia

what does one do love to empty the mind?
'nothing my dear but sit still and be kind'

and how does one conquer the fearing of death?
'by living the minute and counting the breath'

what does one write love when nothing will come?
'write all the bad until you feel it's done'

say, what of the heart and the way that it breaks?
'pour all the dust into what you create'

what do you do when the words are unkind?
'take it to heart and then leave it behind'

oh, who is the man I am trying to be?
'that I don't know dear but one day we'll see'

how can you love me with all that I've done?
'go back to sleep now and wait for the sun'

but how can I sleep with the world in my head?
'write a quick poem and go back to bed'

Ghost Dance

how is your dreaming?
how many cities pass under your feet?
inside your teeth?
spirits in face paint that dance in the heat

feathers on white skin
wrinkles on fingertips
talons on bony hips
opening scars

how are your ears my dear?
burning with words I bet
harsh screeching clarinet
words from afar

how is your dreaming?
how many cities pass under your feet?
tell me how deep
rivers they flow as you're falling asleep?

They

the bleary-eyed and lost in thought
with yellowed fingers, worn and long
from stretching chords and picking nails
I live only with the maddest ones

those whose words need breaking down
like prose discarded, written late
with hair unclean from fingertips
I love those who aren't afraid to hate

the ones whose eyes hide darker thoughts
than you could ever bear to think
the ones who fight them constantly
and often lose, and turn to drink

they who are an inch away
from those who yell out in the throng
or on your bus in fetid rags
I love them here where we belong

you may have fallen once as well
for one such mad one, fond of art
and if so you'll know too well
how efficiently they break your heart

so leave me all, to stew and sit
sleepless here where I belong
in the wake of those I love
here with all the maddest ones

Writer's Block

I am empty, woe is me
void of any poetry

Carnival

a bird told me once to stop drinking
a cricket to 'sing about loss'
a fox said to do much less thinking
a cat called my poetry 'dross'

a badger once said I was dying
and snuck off all smug in the night
a vole said 'you're always denying
the fact that you're losing the fight'

an army of ants on my table
once spelled the words 'you're a hack'
a rat said 'and when you are able...
we'd like all our melodies back'

a wolf at my door called me crazy
and ate up the song on my lips
a stag beetle said I was lazy
but asked me for marketing tips

I swear I once heard a dead rabbit
making light of a painting I'd made
and all of the bees have a habit
of saying I'll never get laid

a crow whispered to me the meaning
of life but then quietly said
maybe my boy you're just dreaming
and this has been all in your head

Oft

I often shook my chains like dew
oft loved the ray the more
but never bettered words of those
who've said it best before

oft wandered lonely as a cloud
oft roved
oft loved and lost and loved at all
but never found the prose

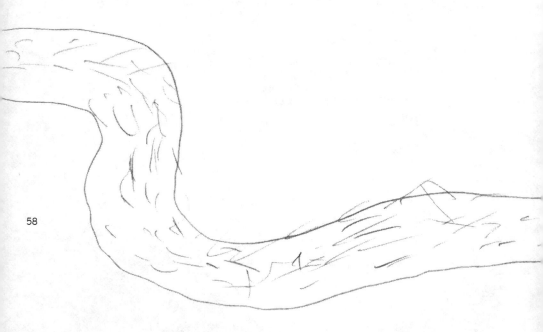

Applaud The Writer

applaud the author, warm indoors
the waking dreamer, nary calm
a rosebud ne'er to open up
with battled mind and withered arm

applaud the poet, out for lunch
all coffee soaked and ink for blood
his dreams now public food for thought
and thought itself that comes as flood

applaud the maker, working late
who lives his life if only to
have something worthy of the words
that he will write and read to you

applaud the writer warm indoors
who plays to play and can but lose
pity he who dares to think
and walk in other people's shoes

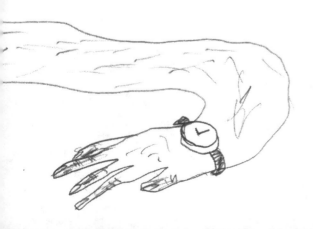

New Year's Eve With Tennyson

this new year's past I spent alone
reading books upon my bed
my mother, midnight, on the phone
and fireworks inside my head

laughing voices I could hear
seemed to join as one and crow
'alone again another year?
you really must get out you know'

so I turned from my old book
to a mostly empty chair
and was relieved as I did look
to see old Alfred sitting there

and I smiled glad to see
(as it's best so I've been told)
that loneliness had company
in such a figure, stern and old

he with cloaked and hatted form
nodded as I rolled my eyes
and with a smile both cold and warm
returned to reading, worn and wise

still outside the clatter raging
I turned back to read my book
and the poet sat, unageing
gave me not a second look

but he breathed like morning waves
and it soothed me till my eyes
softly closed and soon forgave
all the awful joyful cries

and as I fell to needed sleep
I heard him say as he withdrew
in an ancient voice so deep
'sleep well my boy you made it through'

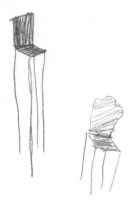

To

to plant flowers
and leave, never to see them grow
to pretend to pretend you're important
but secretly feel that you are
to sleep reluctantly
and believe the hours will miss you
to wake grudgingly
and believe the day has nothing for you
to never dance
and envy those who do
to eat with friends and lovers
to eat alone and taste nothing
to swim
in lonely self importance
to count
to two
and then lose your temper
to be yourself
knowing you do it the best

to live
to pretend you're not dying

to die
and be carried away on the wind

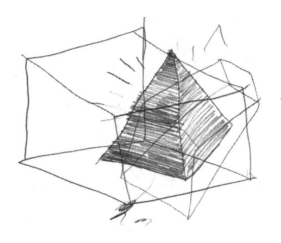

Acknowledgements

With Thanks to Cate, Edwin and
Todd at Eyewear, Liz and Zoe at the
Blair Partnership, and all the humans
who inspire and move me.